Leverage YOU

Leverage YOU

The Road Map to Rediscovering YOU
and Unlocking Your Secret Sauce

CASEY F. MCGEE

For more information, email casey@caseyferrand.com.

Unlock Your Secret Sauce!

As a thank you for reading my book, I want to make it
easier for you to take the next steps to unlock your secret
sauce. Join Leverage You Academy!

Leverage You isn't just about gaining confidence; it's about
becoming the authority you were destined to be. Your
expertise, your story, and your life experiences are your
secret sauce – and it's time to unlock the full flavor.
As a valued member of my community, I'm excited to
offer you a special gift so you can get started today!

Use the code "GrowWithCasey" for 50% off all Leverage
You Academy courses.

Get started today!
https://bit.ly/leverageYOU

This book is dedicated to all of the women who inspired me to dream big and push myself to new heights.

This is also for my family and all of the people who have supported me along the way. A special thank you to the ones who are still with me on this journey and supporting me daily, my husband, son, mom, dad and brothers.

I want to acknowledge the people who have been an integral part of my success. Many of them you will get a chance to read about in the following pages and you will get to understand the impact that they had on me. I would not be where I am without them.

To each of you I say, thank you.

TABLE OF CONTENTS

AN EXCLUSIVE CELEBRITY INTERVIEW WITH CIERA PAYTON

 It's important to have mentors. How can someone find a mentor who can guide them in their personal and professional life?

The first thing that a person should think about is who they want to be or become. Oftentimes we latch on to the ideas of mentors or idolize someone because they radiate what we feel we are lacking. If you want to become a better spouse, mother, artist, leader, etc. ask yourself who or what you need to become in order to achieve that. Where can you use some help in your life to explore incorporating those changes? *Then* start seeking out the mentors. And here's the kicker, you don't always have to have an in-person tangible mentor. I've always loved the idea of virtual mentors, those people that I see from afar, never met, or had a conversation with, but I admire how they do certain things and all that they stand for. It's like using them as a virtual guide to demonstrate the life and person you are aiming to become. Study those people, read their biographies, watch their interviews and take notes.

If you're seeking to connect with an in-person or more tangible mentor, I'd say, still study from them afar first. Get to know what it is that makes them the right mentor for you. Follow them on social media or Linkedin. But before you make your approach, be sure to keep in mind these few things;

1. People are busy living their lives and being that person you look up to. If they don't respond to your message, don't take it personal.

2. They are people too. You might see them out in public and want to say hi and then may not get the response you were looking for (I've been there many times LOL!). Instead of walking away calling them weird or declaring that they were a jerk, just try to offer compassion and keep in mind they are human and are probably battling so much that we aren't aware of.

3. Find out how you can be of service to that person. I would caution reaching out to someone with the only intention of them helping you and catering to your need of mentorship. You can certainly ask for advice and guidance, but offer up ways to achieve this that is convenient for them. You can ask for a 10 - 15 minute zoom discovery call. You can always just start off by messaging or emailing

them a quick note saying that you appreciate what they're contributing to their community/industry/ etc. You can also offer an exchange for time by letting them know that you'd like to gift them a service or some help in exchange for a conversation about (fill in the blank). It's really important to check your intentions and find a way to be of service to those that you desire something from.

4. Then reach out. Keep it nice, professional, and brief!

How have you personally helped people like myself or others as a mentor through the years?

Over the years, I've been fortunate to mentor a diverse group of artists and young individuals, particularly through my involvement with The Michael's Daughter Foundation, a non-profit organization I'm deeply passionate about. A significant portion of my current mentoring efforts is dedicated to the inspiring young minds participating in the foundation's programs. It's incredibly rewarding to witness some of my former students embarking on their college journeys and launching their careers.

My approach to mentorship is rooted in dialogue and understanding. During our occasional lunch meetings, I don't impose my views or dictate what they should do. Instead, I strive to provide a variety of perspectives, tools, and advice drawn from my own experiences. My goal is to empower them to make the best decisions for their unique paths.

In mentoring my peers, I've established an online platform called The In Trive. Here, I share articles, conduct interviews, and offer courses tailored to assist artists in navigating the complexities of their creative careers. Given my busy schedule, this platform allows me to extend guidance and advice efficiently. Through the courses, I provide opportunities for participants to engage in group discussions or one-on-one virtual meetings, ensuring I can address their specific needs.

Working with both my peers and young individuals brings me immense joy. It's always a pleasure to offer guidance and insight to the inspiring minds I encounter, whether they're part of The Michael's Daughter Foundation programs or engage with The In Trive platform. Drawing from my life lessons and experiences in the entertainment industry, I am committed to lending a helping hand in making someone else's journey a little smoother. After all, we all benefit from supporting and uplifting each other in our individual endeavors.

In the book, I discuss the concept of "Secret Sauce." Why is it important for people to leverage their "Secret Sauce-- their skills, talents, and gifts-- in their pursuit of success?

In the world of social media, we're bombarded with the glamorous side of everyone's life, and it's easy to fall into the comparison trap. I'm not exempt—I've totally been there. When I first dipped my toes into acting, agents kept telling me I was "too woman" or not fitting the "high-school-girl-next-door" vibe. So, I tried to "young" myself up, with different hairstyles, pastels, and acting all cutesy.

During my stint working at a Hollywood restaurant, a seasoned actor, a regular customer, became a source of invaluable advice. He was in a bunch of TV series and movies and was always recognized when came in. Most times, he'd sit at the counter where I was often stationed. One day, I mustered the courage to ask him for career advice. And you know what he said? "Change your hair." I was like, huh?! But then he explained, "I see what you're trying to do, but it's not you, that's not your energy." Talk about feeling seen!

It took me a few years to really get a grip on my craft, understand my instrument, and learn how to embrace it fully. My whole self and life experiences have shaped not just my appearance but also how I carry myself. Sure, we can change and level up, but the big lesson from that chat was to embrace what's true to you. You are you, and no one can take that away. Don't try to be something you're not.

All those auditions for high school musical-type roles? Not authentic to me. But the sophisticated, edgy, sensual, and vulnerable gigs that I landed? Those were perfect for me, and they all started rolling in when I embraced my "secret sauce." Being authentic turned out to be the key to unlocking roles that really resonate with the real me.

When you thought about your career at the start, what did you think the pinnacle or the ultimate dream job would be for you? Have you achieved it yet?

When it comes to my career and reaching the pinnacle, I'm still navigating the journey, and, of course, I have dream roles that I'll keep to myself for now—LOL! Maintaining a positive frame of mind and genuinely enjoying the work often leads to moments where God just blows my mind. Many times in my career (and life), it feels like I'm on the verge of taking off, and it's a positive trajectory, not a "starting over" type of scenario. With all that said, I feel that I've achieved a lot, and looking back, I can honestly feel grateful for my life and career. Yet, at the same time, I sense that I'm just getting started.

Was there ever a point when you felt your dream or goals were out of reach, or have you ever felt deterred by circumstances or others in achieving those goals? If so, how did you push past those feelings?

It's all about mindset. What you focus on, you expand. If you find yourself thinking that nothing is working out and others are luckier or more blessed, that energy reflects right back at you. Understanding and applying this concept can be challenging, especially when we carry thought patterns ingrained since childhood. Changing these patterns can seem daunting, but over the years, I've put in the work to retrain my mind.

Whenever I've felt victimized, undermined, or disregarded in my career or life, most of the time, it's because of the thoughts I've been feeding myself. Those thoughts radiate outward, and others respond accordingly. Instead of harboring resentment when someone else lands a role I thought was perfect for me, I shift my thoughts to, "Wow! That's awesome they got that role! Now I know my perfect role is just around the corner. This is putting me one step closer and making me available for mine." It's a simple shift, but we're conditioned to do the opposite—blame, hate, be angry, and afraid. That's a heavy burden to carry.

Don't get me wrong, there are times when I've been disappointed when things haven't worked out as planned. In those moments, I allow myself to feel the disappointment for a day, and then before I know it, I'm dancing in my kitchen to some 80's hits or Funk music, telling myself what I mentioned earlier. I do my best to get back into joy, knowing that what's meant for me is on its way, and joy will expedite its arrival!

> **What were key steps you took along your journey to achieve the success you have in your career and "climb the ladder?"**

My journey boils down to these essential factors:

    a. Ignore the Obstacles: Brush off the obstacles or harsh truths that people may throw your way regarding why you won't succeed. Dodge those people like the plague. If you can't avoid them, pray and visualize their success, showing them unlimited possibilities.

b. Believe and Have Faith: Maintain unwavering faith, no matter what challenges come your way. Cultivate blind and crazy faith, and watch the seemingly impossible transform into the possible.

c. Trust Your Gut: Listen to your gut or that inner voice in your heart. It'll never steer you wrong.

d. Be Bold and Fearless: Don't shy away or dim your light. Be bold and fearless. Shine so brightly that when the spotlight is on you, you illuminate the whole world, empowering others to do the same.

e. Meditate Daily: Don't get too wrapped up in the daily tragedies in the world, instead prioritize daily meditation. Visualize a better place for all. Keep your mind in the right place and your world will reflect that.

f. Respect Your Instrument: Treat your body and mind with respect. Provide your instrument with the right foods, ensure good sleep, and keep it active and healthy.

g. Give and Receive Grace: Extend grace to others and be open to receiving it in return.

All of these things have played a crucial role in steering my life's course. They stand as my guiding principles, and I strive to turn to them whenever things become challenging or when I'm faced with difficulties.

 **Why do you think the readers will enjoy reading this book?**

You are a talented, intelligent, and beautiful light to us all. The knowledge and experience you possess in the journalism and entertainment fields are incomparable. And so, who else better than to write this book. Might I add too, everyone has a story and with it, can teach so many to honor and share theirs. This, my dear friend, you are doing and I have no doubt that you will empower and change lives with the words you have shared.

CHAPTER 1

Facing Failure Head-On

I didn't always enjoy performing and being on television. I was actually a very shy child. So much so that I was extremely quiet around people I didn't know, and still am in some instances as an adult. I think it's my way of getting to know people and feeling out a room before I insert myself or my energy into it. In order to cure me of my shy streak, my mother encouraged me to get into acting. I credit my mother for noticing that about me and finding ways for me to break free of what could have been a crippling fear or hold-up in my life.

I started out as a child actress auditioning for commercials in my hometown of New Orleans and landing some pretty great principal roles. I was featured in commercials for well-known companies like New Orleans Children's Museum, Winn Dixie, Dryades Savings Bank, New Orleans Museum of Art, and Freeport-McMoRan (a Fortune 500 mining company). One of my favorite commercials was for the Louisiana Dairy Association. I had a principal role and it was a major deal to me at the age of eight. I had a featured speaking role at the end of the commercial. I stood there turning a jump rope with friends, then I suddenly stopped and I turned to the camera to deliver my line, "Drink milk!" It took about five or so good takes for me to nail it before they moved on to shooting the next scene. After the commercial started airing, everyone at school called me the "milk girl" from that point on. It was kind of like a badge of honor knowing that people actually saw and remembered me from the commercial.

From there I even auditioned for several movies and eventually auditioned to be a part of a youth theater group called Summer Stages. I remember being so excited and nervous about that audition; later I realized, after being with the group for several years, that the adults in charge didn't require you to have all the talent in the world, but they did require us to be disciplined and professional. Being a part of this theater group was extremely instrumental in my upbringing and fostered my love for performing, being on stage and storytelling. Some of the lessons I learned there are things I've carried with me throughout my life.

I recall struggling to project my voice and feeling so small while standing in the middle of a room surrounded by people or being front and center in the middle of a big stage. It was extremely isolating and intimidating for a nine year old struggling to find her voice. Breaking out of that shell took a little bit of magic from Mikko Machhioni, my theater teacher. He taught me to speak loud enough so MOM or "My Own Magic" could hear me at the back of the theater. Identifying

MOM was exactly what it took for me to speak out, be bold and confident even if I was singing off key.

As someone who often sought validation from others to feel good about myself or to be reassured that I was doing something right, finding my own magic was difficult early on. I was always the child that wanted to make my parents proud, and as the middle child, I tried to be the "good child" who didn't cause trouble or give my parents any reason to seriously discipline me. Performing and being on stage gave me that outlet to be the center of their attention, and I loved it. As an adult, it became easier to find my own magic and it even guided some of my later decisions, from the career decisions I made to the way I wore my hair (more on that later). I grew to love and find value in being my authentic self, and this is something I encourage young women to do any chance I get.

Being under the leadership of Ms. Julie Condy, the founder of Summer Stages, was something I didn't fully appreciate at the time. Ms. Julie was strict on us because this was not just some summer camp to her. For her, this was serious business and she wanted us to be serious every time we walked into a rehearsal room. She was intentional about the work she did with us and did not cut us any slack. We were expected to be on time, be prepared for rehearsals and be present even if our scene wasn't the one being rehearsed. Experiences during those summers with some of the most talented kids I had even met challenged me, molded me and led me to identify early on some of my passions in life.

My first year with Summer Stages was in 1994. I was nine years old and really knew nothing about acting. I just enjoyed telling the stories and learning the lines, songs and dances. My first musical with Summer Stages was called *How to Eat Like a Child* and I had a duet with Grayson. Our song was titled "Waiting," and we were two young kids complaining about always having to wait for our disorganized parents. Every night I sang out in my squeaky nine-year-old voice, projecting so MOM. in the back of the room could hear me, and so my mom sitting in the audience could finally see what I had been practicing for all those nights leading up to show time. Every summer after that, I was eager to get back on that stage. About a week into rehearsals we would have auditions for the lead and supporting roles. This was our chance to shine and show off our skills to land one of those coveted roles or few remaining solo performances. I would always go into it super nervous and filled with anxiety.

I performed with Summer Stages for nine years, and year after year, I landed a starring role or at least a solo in one of the plays. One year we did *Fame the Musical*, and I auditioned for one of the lead roles. At this point I can't even remember which one, but either way I didn't get it and I was devastated. I remember going home the night our parts were announced, bawling my eyes out for hours. I was sixteen at the time and this was likely my first real taste of personal defeat, rejection and disappointment. My mom probably thought I was crazy as she tried to console me and calm me down. To me it was the biggest heartbreak in my life. "I'm not the lead. I'm in the chorus. How could that be? I'm always the lead or at least get a solo!" Those were the thoughts running through my head. It was like the end of the world to me because that role was something I really wanted and not only did I not get it, I got nothing! I eventually stopped crying and went to school the next day with these huge swollen eyes from my hours of crying. Yet, I eventually realized, even though I was a pretty good singer, dancing was never my strong suit and the role went to the person who was better suited for the part.

I recently recalled this experience while working with a coach and realized how momentous a moment it was that has played out in other areas and life decisions throughout my life. That one brush with what I felt was rejection shaped future choices like my college, career and likely bad relationships I got into as well. It's like I ultimately stopped going for what I really wanted in life and even settled for some things because I did not want to feel rejected or like I wasn't good enough ever again. I made choices based on what I knew I was guaranteed to get, or I chose partners where I really knew I was worthy of much better. I allowed myself to settle for the next best thing, the chorus, when I really knew I was always meant to be the lead. I'm not saying the path and life I've created for myself haven't been filled with accomplishments and amazing experiences, but I do wonder where life could have led if I didn't let one past feeling of rejection shape how I viewed myself and my abilities.

Ultimately my time with Summer Stages did lead me to my future career path. My first memory of being in the newsroom was when I was about twelve years old. I was there performing with some of the kids from Summer Stages as we were promoting our upcoming show. I remember being in the news studio at WWL TV waiting to perform on the morning news show. There was so much anticipation waiting behind the scenes, seeing the lights and big cameras and watching the news anchors do their jobs. That's when I believe the news bug first hit me, although I didn't know it yet.

All throughout high school, I was extremely active. I played volleyball and softball, ran on the track team, even tried soccer for a year, cheerleading, sang in the concert choir, the church choir, played clarinet in the concert band. I did the yearbook club, Beta Club, was a class officer and was on the homecoming court every year. And in the summers I still did plays. My eighth- and twelfth-grade years I also attended New Orleans Center for Creative Arts (NOCCA) where I studied musical theater. I kept my mom pretty busy as well, running me from school to some rehearsal or audition or competition. There was always something going on and Mom and Dad always kept up and showed up.

By my senior year of high school, it was time to start making some decisions for the future. Up until that point, I tried nearly everything I could or wanted to do, but now it was time to make decisions that would set the stage for the future me. I could either be a nurse like my mom and grandmother, but then I remembered that one time I went to work with my mom and they were amputating a man's toe. I couldn't handle the blood, so I thought, "Maybe the medical field isn't for me."

Then there was acting, which I'd always loved and was pretty good at and could grow to be better at if I really focused on it. But I thought, "Do I want to face years of auditioning for roles and the possibility of repeated rejection and disappointment?" There was this aptitude test that my mom took for me (don't ask me how that works, I guess she just really knew her child that well), and it said I would be good in fields like teaching and journalism. "That's it! That's what I'll do!" I had always loved writing; I aced all my English papers in high school and I made a 32 on the ACT in the English category, so I chose journalism as my major.

The next major decision was where I'd go to college. As a senior at NOCCA, all of the seniors went to Chicago to audition for theater schools from colleges around the country all in one place. I looked at the list of universities and conservatories around the country that would be there and picked out a handful that I wanted to audition for, including places like Ithaca in New York, Carnegie Mellon University, University of Miami and Southern Methodist University in Dallas, Texas. I picked all of these places because they were in cities I thought I'd love to live in. I only applied to two colleges in the state of Louisiana and only one in New Orleans: McNeese State University and Loyola University.

Then the acceptance letters started coming. I got accepted into the University of Miami's theater program, which was ranked one of the top fifty in the country. I was ecstatic and thought, "Maybe I really am good at this acting thing." My parents and I packed up our RV and drove sixteen hours to Miami to see the campus and the city. I absolutely loved everything about it; the campus felt like what sixteen-year-old me thought college should feel like. It was huge, beautiful and in MIAMI. Then it was getting closer to the end of the school year and I got another acceptance letter from SMU. They didn't accept me into the theater program but did offer me an academic scholarship. It wasn't my first choice, but they were offering me more money than Miami and I definitely didn't want my parents taking on a huge bill. So I chose SMU and I'd major in journalism. I arrived on campus for freshman orientation in August having never set foot on the campus before.

It turned out to be a great choice. The journalism program there was ranked in the top 10 percent in the United States and in the top five journalism schools in Texas. It taught me all the fundamentals of news, introduced me to some of the people I looked up to in the news business and set me on the path toward becoming a journalist. One of our responsibilities as journalism majors was logging hours with the daily morning news program called *The Daily Update* and writing for the campus newspaper. I logged dozens of hours each semester working at SMU-TV, waking up before the sun to work with my classmates to write, produce and record a thirty-minute show. Seeing us budding journalists do this process every morning was so exhilarating. I felt at home in that college newsroom and knew I was headed down the right path.

Throughout those early years of making decisions for myself I learned some major life lessons that shaped the future me. The biggest lesson for me was being **disciplined** in everything you do. It takes a lot for a child to remain disciplined, but being in those rehearsal rooms instilled in me self control, responsibility and that there were consequences for my bad actions or choices. As adults we have to be disciplined to leverage up in our journey because a disciplined person follows the rules and has a standard of behavior that helps them maintain self-control and has an ability to set and successfully achieve goals.

Throughout these experiences, I also gained **independence**. There was no one in my family who had taken the path I was embarking upon. All the women I looked up to were nurses, so I had no one to really show me the way on the journey I was taking. I was forced to be independent in order to achieve my personal goals. In this growth journey you will have to become self-sufficient because you'll likely be on your path alone. There may not be people around you who understand the journey you are on or be able to show you the path to take. You may be completely alone as you chart your course, but you'll grow stronger in that independence and you'll find strength in taking control of your own destiny.

Although I avoided failure and rejection in some of the decisions I made, I became very **decisive** and **determined** in my decision making. Once I made up my mind about doing something, I was going to do whatever it took for me to succeed at that. The same must be true for you. You can not hesitate to call the shots and must be determined in your pursuit of achieving your goals. You cannot compromise your standards or beliefs to do so, and will have to make sacrifices to achieve those goals.

Now I want you to think about how you may be letting your fear of failing or a lack of discipline stop you from achieving your goals or moving into the next level of your career or progressing on your journey. Stop letting those fears, doubts or uncertainties paralyze you and hinder you from living in your purpose.

REFLECTION ⟩⟩⟩

Failure is a natural part of life, but it's not the failure that defines you—it's how you define your failure. Do you let your failure completely paralyze you, throw you off course and get you stuck in a place of despair? Or do you let your failure motivate you and push forward in life? It's OK to feel your failure—the pain, the regret and the letdown. Use that energy, learn from it and move on to live another day. How long do you allow yourself to sit in your failure? How do you get back on track after facing failure? How do you allow failure to shape your future goals?

1. What goals did you set for yourself early on?

_____

_____

_____

_____

_____

2. Have you reached those goals?

_____

_____

_____

_____

_____

3. If so, what steps did you take to achieve them?

_____

_____

_____

_____

_____

4. If not, how can you start making steps now to achieve them?

_____

_____

_____

_____

_____

CHAPTER 2

Just Get in the Door

August 29, 2005, is a day that is permanently etched in the minds of most New Orleans natives. We know where we were, who we were with and most of all what we lost. For the rest of the country, I imagine August 29 is just the start of their countdown to a three-day Labor Day weekend but for me it was life altering. I had just started my second year of college. It was a Monday morning and I was in one of my journalism classes. As expected, we were required to be up to date on current events, and what better way to be sure we are staying abreast of the latest news and headlines than a pop quiz? Our professor started the quiz with this question, "What US city is currently being hit by a hurricane?"

Of course I knew the answer. I'd been up all night watching news reports and feeling so far removed from the city I knew and loved. It was about 9 a.m. in Dallas, Texas, and I hadn't heard from my parents and brothers all night. All I knew was they planned to evacuate, but I wasn't sure where they were going. Each time I tried calling, there was no answer and the phone would not even ring. So, when my professor asked the question, the answer rang in my head, but I never wrote it down. I couldn't hold in the stress, anxiety and worry any longer, and I burst into tears and ran into the restroom. I'm sure my professor was stunned and had no clue what was wrong with this frail college student crying and running out of her class, but I assume my classmates clued her in.

Every year when hurricane season came around, if we needed to evacuate we would pack little more than a few pairs of clothes—although Mom always grabbed a plastic bin stuffed with important documents and photos before we headed downtown to a high-rise office building where my uncle worked or maybe we would drive to a hotel far enough from harm's way. Sometimes we wouldn't even leave, we'd hunker down upstairs and wait for the worst of it to pass, but this was different. It felt different. I felt alone.

Finally, later that day, I heard from my mom and relief filled my body. She told me they'd made it to Dallas and would be staying for a few days. We sat in a cousin's small apartment and watched the news reports together for hours and could not look away. Seeing pictures of familiar streets and landmarks streamed across the air, and even watching my local newscasters deliver reports in the midst of the destruction was gut-wrenching and earth-shattering. I kept watching, hoping I would see something that showed me something remotely close to my home because I needed to know if our home was OK.

My parents eventually made their way back to New Orleans once it was safe. We had nearly two feet of water inside our house. It would be months before I made it back to see our home in person over a holiday break. My dad described it to me and showed me pictures, but seeing it first-hand was so unreal. My old neighborhood was deserted because many people didn't return home or they simply moved away. Inside our home, half of the walls were gutted on the bottom floor because the water had come up that high. There was still a lingering moldy smell throughout the house and the entire city that reminded you of what had happened only months prior.

Many stores and businesses had yet to reopen, including my mother's business that she ran with my grandmother. But my family was not making plans to reopen. By then, my mother, two brothers and my mother's parents had relocated to Ruston, a town in North Louisiana. My mom and younger brother were living at Lincoln Parish Park in our RV and he had enrolled in high school there. My dad was living in the second story of our house in New Orleans while he picked up odd jobs to continue supporting our family. He hated being away for months on end, but that was the way our family existed for a year or more. I was still in college in Dallas, so I drove four hours to Ruston over holiday breaks or whenever I could, and stayed in the RV with my mom and younger brother. It was strange existing in this way, but this was our new home for the time being.

I spent the summer after Hurricane Katrina working as an intern at WDSU News in New Orleans. I spent a brief stint there as an unofficial intern the prior summer. My dad was able to get me access because he cut grass for Norman Robinson, a longtime anchor and staple at the station. I did not do much that first summer because I was still a little timid and unsure of myself. Plus, here I was working directly with the news reporters and anchors I'd grown up watching. I felt like I wanted to stay out of their way and just observe, and that's exactly what I did. I mostly sat on the assignment desk helping to answer phones and field calls from viewers who wanted the news to cover their story.

In order to get the internship the following summer, I had to write an essay about why I wanted to be there. I wish I could see that essay today to recall what I wrote and why I was selected to be one of the twelve or so interns that semester. I remember getting the email that I had been selected and bursting with excitement. Even though I had spent some time there the summer before, this time it felt like I truly earned my place there and it wasn't because my dad knew someone. Although in a few short years I would learn that having connections would be a huge asset in this business.

When I started working at WDSU the summer after my junior year, I wanted to jump right into things. Since I had gotten my feet wet the summer before, I felt like I knew the ropes and was more comfortable being in the newsroom and around some of the people I'd come to know. It had been an extremely busy time in news covering the aftermath and rebuilding efforts in New Orleans city immediately following the hurricane and there was no shortage of stories to cover.

At the time, my father and I were living in a FEMA trailer behind the business my mother previously owned because he was working on reconstructing the first floor of our house after tearing the floors and sheetrock out of it due to the water damage. I'd spend two to three days a week at the news station. I did not want to waste my time there or waste any of their time. I needed to learn as much as I could, I needed to take this time to grow and I had to get material to eventually put on my résumé tape. I think I was required to clock at least 120 hours over the course of the summer, but I ended with somewhere closer to 150. I treated it like a job because to me it was, and it was a valuable time.

That summer I worked closely with the producers, especially Amy Sneed, who was also the intern coordinator. She was tough on us and expected a lot. I think mostly because she hand selected each one of us and didn't want us embarrassing her. At the beginning of our three-month internship, Amy gave us a packet filled with questions and things we needed to learn during the course of our time there. We had to be able to name all of the on-air talent and newsroom staff. We also had to know technical news terminology, current events and local politicians. I always give credit to Amy for allowing me to get my start in the business. That time gave me the opportunity to be in a position to learn from some of the best in the business and from people I admired including her.

I took full advantage! I would make beat calls in the morning, calling all of the law enforcement agencies and fire departments at the beginning of a shift to find out if they were working any cases or incidents. I would read wire copy to write stories for producers. I went out in the field with photographers to interview people and I'd write those stories too. I sometimes shadowed Camille Whitworth and Drew McAllister, a dynamic duo in the field. Being able to work so closely with two news veterans taught me so much, from the art of writing a compelling news package to delivering a great live shot. Those two were fun to work with and also became great mentors for me as I progressed throughout my career.

Drew helped me shoot a number of reporter stand-ups that ended up on my first real résumé tape. He also taught me how to do linear editing, which is basically recording video clips from one tape onto another to create a completely edited package or news story. Those techniques are no longer used in the business because of the advancements in technology, but learning that skill set, which I never learned in college, proved to be vital when I eventually got my first job in the business. We'll get to that later though.

I finished that summer by helping Amy field produce a live broadcast from the site of one of the levee breaches that flooded a section of the city. We were coming up to the one-year anniversary of Hurricane Katrina and the news team produced a special broadcast commemorating the anniversary. The main anchors, Norman Robinson and Kriss Fairbairn, were doing all of the evening newscasts live from the industrial canal, detailing the lingering impact of the storm and the little progress that had been made since then. It was a proud moment being on the team that helped produce those shows, and I watched in amazement as they broadcast live from a location that led to so much devastation. By the end of that summer internship, Amy told me I was a star intern. I felt like it too. I learned and did a lot, all of which helped mold me and make me feel more confident when I returned to SMU for my final year of college.

Thinking back on this time, I don't really focus on the tragedy of it all. I am reminded of all the ways my life became better and my journey became more meaningful. It's said that people who endure tragedy are often the most successful. Hurricane Katrina was the biggest tragedy of my lifetime that had a direct impact on me. I'd seen the terrorist attacks on 9/11 and remember watching it all unfold in amazement after our teacher rolled in a television for us to watch the news in my 10th grade Geometry class. This changed our way of life in America. When Katrina changed my life, we didn't stay in a state of despair, we picked up and moved forward.

We all endure some type of hardship in life and those hard times can make us want to give up and back down. But tragedy can also teach us things and motivate us to move forward leading to some of our greatest personal successes. Sometimes being pulled backward can propel us forward. Being knocked off course, led to a personal season of success. But what does it take to turn these tragedies and hardships into our success stories? It takes three things: dreaming, passion and persistence.

DREAMING

During our deepest despair in the midst of our most challenging times, there are only a few things that we can hold on to — one of them is a dream. We find hope in thinking about our future, thinking about what's on the other side of this and holding onto the idea of being able to say "I made it." That is exactly what helps us to push through the present challenges and guide us to a place where we will again find joy and satisfaction in life. Just like my tragedy pushed me to my passion, the same can be true for you. Allow your tragedy be the thing that points you in the right direction toward your passion. Your hardship can create a vision for your life that makes us want to get up and pursue it every day. Even in your place of pain and suffering, there is something to look forward to as a means of motivation. Use that to propel you forward, build upon and live for.

PERSISTENCE

Adversity can teach us so many lessons that stick with us throughout our lives, and one of the most valuable traits is persistence. If the tragedy I endured taught me anything, it's that giving up is never an option. You truly gain the most by persisting and persevering through the roughest challenges. It doesn't matter how many times you're forced to persist, you can't stop persisting, you can't take no for an answer and you can't be turned away from achieving your goal. If you don't give up during your most challenging times, there is no way you will throw in the towel and give up when things are going your way.

PASSION

Even in the midst of the challenging times, don't make excuses as to why you can't do something. In the midst of my family losing everything we had and the only home I ever knew, I could have easily crawled into a hole and used that as an excuse to take a break from college and allow myself time to grieve with my family, but instead I became relentless in pursuing my passion. You too can allow the worst of times to drive you deeper into your passion, Become so passionate about what you are doing that it no longer seems like a challenge. Through all that you endure, seek to balance that by doing what you love. In pursuing your passion, never pursue it with a lackluster effort. There is nothing more rewarding than looking back and knowing you gave it your all.

REFLECTION

As we navigate through life, we are faced with challenges big and small. The magnitude of them may not be evident at the time, but they can weigh heavily on the trajectory of your future. What was that first big tragedy for you—the thing that took you off course, the thing that shattered your dreams and made you give up?

1. What are your desires?

_____

_____

_____

_____

2. What have you always wanted to do or be?

_____

_____

_____

_____

_____

3. Why didn't you pursue those desires?

_____

_____

_____

_____

_____

CHAPTER 3

Landing My FIRST Real Job

*"You've been rejected by jobs you felt you could've fit in, but
God is preparing you for a job that you will stand out in."*
-Ifeanyi Imachukwu

When I graduated college, I had no job prospects on the horizon while some of the other students in my classes were already landing jobs or at least being called for interviews. Even though I'd just completed four years of college and earned two degrees, I still lacked confidence in my abilities as a budding journalist.

I was going through the motions of crafting my résumé and making sure it highlighted everything I did during my summer internships. I knew one thing for sure: If I wanted to catch the attention of a news director in hopes of getting an interview, I had to show them what I was truly capable of because my doctored-up résumé was not going to cut it. I worked for hours pulling together stand-ups (ten-second clips of me standing and talking or doing the quintessential aimless reporter walk to nowhere), editing and reediting stories to make my résumé tape, which I knew was going to be the only way I could showcase what I could do.

At that time, reporters still submitted VHS or DVD copies of résumé tapes to news directors to apply for available jobs in cities they had never heard of. Once I finally got my résumé tape ready for public consumption, I solicited some support from Dennis Joseph (DJ), a family friend who helped me make dozens of VHS tapes that I would mail out to news directors all across the south. The New Orleans girl had no plans on being too far from home.

I scoured the Internet, searching websites of news stations from Texas to Florida looking for any available jobs. I came up with a list of at least a dozen jobs that I wanted to apply for that I either thought I had a chance at getting or were within driving distance of my family. I printed my résumé on the nicest paper I could find, made labels, dropped those bulky VHS tapes inside large manila envelopes and put them in the mail. By now it was the end of summer and I went weeks without hearing from anyone and figured I wouldn't get a call at all.

I knew the odds of getting a job in news were slim because the competition is stiff. It seemed so unlikely, that I started looking for other career opportunities. I applied for Teach for America, even though I never once considered that as a profession. When I got a big fat NO from TFA, it was another huge blow to my confidence. What was I going to do? No one wants to take a chance on an inexperienced college grad, I thought.

At this time I was back in New Orleans, living in a FEMA trailer with my dad and really started questioning my future. Then, it came! The first call was for a job as a news reporter in Alexandria, Louisiana. This was it! This was my chance to at least speak to a news director and convince him that I was capable of doing the job. I jumped in my black Mustang and hit the road so fast. I went in for the interview with a new dose of confidence and showed them I was ready and willing to work.

Weeks passed and I didn't hear anything, and I realized I wasn't going to hear from them. I then decided I had to be more proactive. At the time, my mother and brothers were living in a small town in North Louisiana. They evacuated to Ruston, LA following Hurricane Katrina and made a home. Several of the news stations I'd submitted my work to were within an hour of them, so I decided to make the drive up there.

I took to the road determined to make my way into someone's office to speak about a job. Although I'd already mailed my résumé and tape to all of these places, I decided to personally go to each of the news stations in Monroe, Louisiana, to hand deliver my materials in hopes of being able to conveniently get a chance to meet the news directors in person. I showed up to the first station, which was my first choice of where I wanted to work, and I got nowhere. Then on to the next station where I asked to speak to the news director and was told he wasn't available. I left my information with the receptionist hoping she'd actually get it to him and returned home yet again feeling defeated.

The next day I received a call from that news director asking me to come in for an interview. "This is it," I thought, "my first big break to set me on the path to becoming a real journalist!" I was so eager for the interview that I would have driven there the very same day to meet him. When I did go in, I sat down with Randall Kamm, and the first thing I noticed when I walked into his office was the boxes of VHS tapes cluttered in the corner. I couldn't help but wonder if the tape I'd mailed months ago was somewhere buried in this pile where tapes clearly went to die and never be seen again.

I took every opportunity I could to tell Randall why I was perfect for the job and reassured him that even though I just graduated from college, I had the knowledge and experience from my internship that was invaluable. Would you believe that he hired me on the spot? Neither could I! He told me he could only offer me a salary of $20,000 a year. I didn't care about the salary; I wanted the job and I got it. I went home elated and shared the news with my family.

When I went in for my first day of work the following week, I was ready to prove to Randall that he made the right decision in taking a chance on me. Little did I know, Randall didn't feel like he was "taking a chance," but he instead knew he was making a good hire. He revealed to me that day that he knew I'd be a great reporter because I was "tenacious" enough to come there in person and get the job I wanted. He said it was clear to him that I was the kind of person who was willing to do what it takes to find a story and would go the extra mile to get what I needed to get the job done. Up until that day, I had no idea what tenacious even meant, but at that moment I knew that tenacity was going to take me far. To top it off, Randall also gave me a raise on that first day, so instead of making $20,000 a year, I was going to make $21,000. Yes, it was still pennies, but I earned every cent of it.

After searching for months and months for a job at any news station that would take me, I finally landed a job when I bet on myself. When I earned the internship at WDSU, they bet on me. They obviously saw something in me that was worth investing in because the anchors spent the entire summer pouring all of their knowledge and skills into me. When I walked into Randall Kamm's office that afternoon in August, he bet on me. It was time for me to start betting on myself. I spent years perfecting my craft and getting ready for a moment like this. It was time for me to step into what I knew that I was more than capable of.

Yes, I had experienced some extremely disappointing rejections while in the process of trying to get my foot in the door, but I didn't let those rejections stop me from going after what I knew I was called to do.

What if I would have gotten that job at Teach or America, and taken an entirely different career route? I would have been extremely unhappy because I was just going for it because I started to doubt that what I really wanted was attainable. Don't let rejection get you off of your path. Yes, you may stumble a bit if you experience rejection. No one likes rejections, it's not fun for anyone but let that rejection fuel you. Being rejected from Teach for America was one of the best things that happened to me because it would have taken me down a path that was not for me.

Sometimes rejection is just a way to protect you from what's not for you. It's a way to push you closer towards that opportunity that is right for you.

REFLECTION ≫≫

Despite the rejections and adversity we face in life, we cannot let them define us. Those things should not discourage you to a point of giving up on yourself, your dream or your passion. You define who you are, who you want to be and the goals you have for your future. Do not let the fear of failure kill your purpose and desire before you give yourself a chance to reach your goal. It's true—nothing beats a failure but a try. How do you respond in the face of rejection and adversity? Does fear of failure keep you from following your heart?

1. Why are you doing what you're currently doing?

_____

_____

_____

_____

_____

2. What do you wish you made more time to do?

_____

_____

_____

_____

_____

3. What about your work makes you feel valued?

_____

_____

_____

_____

_____

CHAPTER 4

I Want to QUIT

N ow that I'd made it in the door, it was time to show up and do the work. I was scheduled to work from 2:30–10:30 p.m., but every morning was spent searching for stories for the day. Each day when I got to work, we had an afternoon editorial meeting to determine story assignments for each reporter. Each of us was required to come to the meeting with at least three possible story ideas that we could work on that day. The goal was to find stories that could lead the newscast so you could be first in the show. The hardest thing about that was finding stories that had the potential to be a great headline in a small city where not much was happening. The cat stuck in a tree was not going to cut it, not unless the cat turned out to be a wild cat of some sort that was threatening children and pets in the neighborhood.

I woke up at 8 or 9 every morning, searching newspapers and news websites to find the three stories I would pitch at the meeting that afternoon. I made beat calls to police and fire departments like I learned to do during my internship hoping it would produce something of substance that was worth reporting on later that afternoon. I even searched national news to find any story that could be localized to become relevant to people in our market. I relied on everything I learned about the rules of journalism to find stories that were timely, relevant, of human interest and had conflict or controversy.

Each day, I walked into the newsroom ready for the afternoon meeting with three story ideas that I knew would fit the bill. I met the mark on most days, but of course it's the days that I didn't that stand out more. My assignment editor had a way of making this huge ball of knots form in the pit of my stomach every time it was my turn to give my story pitches. You see, Phil Duckworth was seasoned and like a drill sergeant who had a way of making us fresh-out-of-college news reporters feel totally inept. As I went through my story ideas one by one, that ball of knots in my stomach would get bigger as "Sergeant Duckworth" would give me this look of disdain as he shot down each one. Eventually, it got to the point that I was dreading going to work every day. Some days I even cried on the way to work because I just knew not one of the stories I found would be good enough.

On top of the stress of finding stories, I had small-market blues from working in West Monroe, Louisiana. Every day when I arrived at work, I was greeted by the horrible smells emitting from the nearby paper mill that seeped into our second-floor newsroom around the same time every day. The other issue with working in a small news market is that a lot of the equipment is not in the best working order, which can make doing the job that much harder. There were many times my story was late making it on air, which is a huge no-no in this business, because I was still learning to operate the equipment. Outside of the struggles at work, I was also facing problems before I even set foot in the door sometimes. I lived with my parents about thirty minutes away from the news station, and I had a propensity for driving too fast. I was getting speeding tickets on the way to work on nearly a monthly basis. You'd think I would have learned my lesson after the second or third time, but no! I just kept pushing the limits.

After about seven months of working at KTVE, I had reported on some pretty big stories, conducted some stellar interviews and even got tasered for a story. I should probably give you some more context on how that came about. I was invited by the local police department to do a story about some of the training the officers go through to prepare them for their jobs. One of the things they do for training is get tasered so they can know what it feels like to be tased should they ever have to discharge their taser gun on a suspect.

As I stood by watching each person one by one take a shock from the taser gun, my curiosity was piqued. I wondered if it was as bad as they made it seem, or were they putting on a show for our cameras? Then someone asked me if I wanted to try it myself. The adventurous side of me couldn't say no, so I decided I would creatively incorporate myself being tasered into my story in a stand-up (a stand-up is when a television reporter appears in front of the camera to narrate part of a story—most often at the beginning to set up the story or in the middle to add context).

They asked if I wanted the one-, two- or three-second charge, and I agreed to take a one-second charge. Two officers stood on either side of me to hold me up as I prepared for the shocking moment. I practiced what I would say in my stand-up, so I could do it and get tased all in one take. I definitely did not want to do this more than once. When it was go time, I said my stand-up and the shock went through my body. I lost all muscle control, my body slumped over, and the officers had to hold me up until feeling returned to my legs. When my photographer and I finished shooting the story, our assignment editor called to tell us we needed to do another assignment.

A truck carrying timber lost some of its load causing major damage and injuring other drivers. This would certainly be the lead story for the evening newscasts. This also meant the stand-up I shot would likely never see the light of day. After reporting on the log truck crash for the evening newscasts, I stayed late to write and edit my previous story about the officer training. When I went back to look at the stand-up I shot earlier in the day, I realized the photographer's camera was completely out of focus. I guess he was not focused on doing his job while I was being shocked in the back. Although the quality of the stand-up was not great at all, I fought tooth and nail to make sure that it would make it on air that night. I couldn't have done all of that for nothing and let the only memory of that moment be the burns on my butt and shoulder that remained for months.

While my time in Monroe was filled with many highlights, it seemed the low points overshadowed it all because there I was again feeling like this was not the career for me. It was then that the next opportunity came when a job opened up in Shreveport, Louisiana, to replace a longtime education reporter at KTBS News. I applied but did not expect to get it because it was at one of the stations I previously applied to right out of college. I questioned whether I had what it took after only eight months in the business and I questioned whether this was a career path I wanted to continue on.

When I received a call from Randy Bain, the news director, to do an interview, I was more than surprised. We spoke and he expressed interest in hiring me for the job, but something in me was not willing or excited to accept it and I openly expressed that to him. I told him how rough the last eight months had been working with equipment that often failed, missing deadlines because of slow editors and how I struggled coming up with daily story ideas. After hearing me out, he still encouraged me to stick with it because, as he put it, those were "small market issues," and he asked me to consider giving it another shot in Shreveport before deciding to leave the business altogether. Plus, he said I was too good to give up on it quite yet and he was sure I would grow to love the job more working in a larger city.

That pep talk was just what I needed to see the value in myself and regain my confidence. Someone who didn't know me and saw maybe five minutes of my work was able to see something in me that I clearly wasn't seeing in myself. Once I accepted the fact that I was really becoming good at doing the job and was more frustrated with the things that made doing the job a challenge, I fully embraced taking the new job and making the move to Shreveport to give it another shot.

Having confidence and belief in myself was a constant struggle especially after repeated rejections. Why is it so important to believe in yourself? Believing in yourself means being able to trust yourself to do what you say you will and can do. It also means knowing that the efforts you put into doing what you say you will do will eventually lead to the desired outcomes.

When you believe in yourself, you can overcome self-doubt and have the confidence to take the necessary steps to get things done. Even if you have all of the skills, training, and experience in the world, you can still be paralyzed by fear and self-doubt that can make success feel out of your grasp. Developing positive self-esteem is key to believing in your capability to achieve and contribute to the world whatever you set out to. It means knowing that your ideas, feelings, and opinions have worth. Of course, you'll never fully rid yourself of doubts, but developing a healthy dose of self-esteem will help you overcome them.

REFLECTION

Life will be full of setbacks, roadblocks and distractions that can take us off course and even make us lose sight of the course we have mapped out for ourselves. When obstacles stand in our way, we have a choice to make. Do we let them stop us or do we push through to achieve our goals? It can be far too easy to want to give up and quit because it's too hard, too complicated or taking too long to achieve your goals. When challenges and adversities come, now is the time to go into overdrive, work harder, dig deeper and practice persistence. It will make you so much better and stronger once you're on the other side.

1. What are some of the obstacles that have taken you off course?

   _____

   _____

   _____

   _____

   _____

2. What would it take to get you back on course to achieve your goals?

   _____

   _____

   _____

   _____

3. What is one thing you can start doing today to get back on track?

_____

_____

_____

_____

_____

CHAPTER 5

Doing it ALL

Over the course of my career and my life, as I have come to realize, I mastered the skill of doing it all. Growing up, I was involved in every extracurricular activity possible at my school. It was a small school with maybe two hundred students in seventh through twelfth grades, so if you were the type of person to get involved in school activities, you got involved in a lot of them. And if you showed even a little bit of athleticism, you didn't just play one sport, you played two, three or all sports. Throughout my time in high school, I was on the volleyball (my favorite), softball, soccer and track teams. I was also in the concert choir and concert band (I played clarinet), in the Beta Club and National Honor Society, on the yearbook staff and homecoming court all four years, and I was a cheerleader. It makes my head spin thinking about all the activities I was involved in and wondering how my parents even managed my busy schedule with two other kids in the house.

No one told me I had to do all these things, I was just able to do them all fairly well so I fit it all in as best I could. I never reached my full potential in any sport because I was so busy doing them all and never focused on just one. Even when I was active in musical theater, which includes equal measures of acting, dancing and singing skills, I don't believe I fully mastered any of these. I was good enough though to land leading roles in a number of productions.

As a journalist, there came a point where I was expected to do it all. While working in Shreveport in 2008 during a recession, we saw a lot of change happen in our newsroom. The station was cutting back and even had a massive layoff of possibly sixteen people including some longtime newsroom staff. It was a tough time for many of us because what that meant for those of us remaining was the expectation of continuing to get the same number of shows and stories on the air with fewer people involved. It meant reporters had to start performing the role of the photojournalists and vice versa. Instead of being able to focus solely on writing a good story and making it on air for the evening news, I also had to start shooting my own video and editing all of my own stories. Reporters were training videographers how to write news copy and they were training us how to use the cameras and editing software.

We were trained and indoctrinated with the concept of "doing more with less." That phrase became the bane of our existence and we dreaded hearing those words on a daily basis. It felt like some corporate jargon being fed to us that was meant to inspire us to keep pounding out the work, but we started to grow weary and worn out. But soon, with a slight change in perspective, I began to see it as an opportunity. I began to feel empowered by my ability to do it all for myself and not need a photographer. I even became a better storyteller as my photojournalism skills improved because I was able to write my stories based on the video I knew I shot and the visuals really became an asset to tell the stories. All of the new skills I was learning along the way also increased my knowledge of the job, my value to my current and future employers and my confidence in myself. On top of that, the company was investing in training for us to hone the skills needed to succeed at taking on the new roles as multimedia journalists.

Three years spent working in Shreveport, honing my craft and learning more skills gave me the confidence to start applying for and land a job in one of the top ten news markets in the country. I went from a small city to working in Houston, Texas, as a multimedia journalist where I stayed for a year before landing my goal job in New Orleans as a reporter at the local NBC affiliate. Landing a job at WDSU in New Orleans was a huge milestone moment for me, but we'll get into more of that in the next chapter.

Future career moves put me in a position to be the director of communications at a growing nonprofit in New Orleans where I played a pivotal role in developing a highly productive communications team and being a spokesperson for the organization. That was all a result of being forced to do it all, learn new things and growing at each level of my career.

Now, what this all means is that because I have grown so good at doing it all, I sometimes get caught up in doing too much. I find myself getting very busy doing work for my clients, working on my business, hosting and emceeing events all over, acting in television and film projects, being a full-time wife and mom and maintaining my schedule of spiritual meetings and still trying to make time for myself to take care of myself mentally and physically. I can tell when I'm trying to do too much because it starts to take a toll on me mentally and has a way of slowing down my productivity.

If you've ever heard the saying, "a jack of all trades is a master of none," it may have a negative connotation in your mind. But did you know that phrase was historically used to describe THE William Shakespeare who, before becoming a famous playwright, was always hanging around theaters helping with the stage, set and costumes, remembering lines and trying to direct? The full phrase is actually "a jack of all trades is a master of none, but oftentimes better than a master of one." This was meant as a compliment. The truth is, along the way it has helped me in four key areas: self-discovery, time management, setting boundaries and developing curiosity.

Self-discovery

Being a "jack of all trades" has proven to be essential for my personal growth and professional success. Trying and doing a lot of things has been critical for my self-discovery, helping me discover who I am and determine what my strongest skills are. It has helped me easily identify my own strengths and weaknesses. For instance, when I tried soccer in high school, I only played for one season because I quickly realized it wasn't the sport for me. I was not a fan of running around a field chasing after a ball for a long time in the cold.

Time management

This has also helped me become really good at managing my time. I have found it extremely helpful to plan using block scheduling, which makes it possible for me to be more productive. This means setting aside a specific block of time to do really focused work on one task. The level of productivity that comes from this is so powerful. I've also grown really good at finishing assignments just in the knick of time. I can remember reviewing my essays or writing assignments with my mother in my college dorm room only minutes before they were due. This also showed up when I managed to get reports filed minutes before being live on air.

Setting boundaries

As for setting boundaries, I only work with clients that I feel I will enjoy working with and will have a good rapport. If the thought of working with someone induces feelings of stress and anxiety, it is a client I will usually decline to work with or limit the amount of time I need to engage with that client. This is why it has been really helpful for me to hone in on identifying my ideal client and being clear about who I serve as a publicist..

Strength in curiosity

As a journalist, I am a naturally curious person, which is why I have explored so many things in my life and career. I covered so many stories on so many different topics and learned so many things through the years that I used to say I "knew a little about a lot." Being curious about my world and my work made me better at doing it. I set up my media coaching and consulting business in a way that allows me to take everything I've learned through my experiences to help others build their brands and businesses. As a creative, I love variety and don't like being bound to doing just one thing. I am one of those people who is always looking for opportunities for personal and professional advancement by exploring deeper, learning more and discovering. It can leave one a bit frazzled, but all the knowledge I've gained comes in handy. I'm never bored because there is always something for me to do. I can have an impact on so many people's lives in various sectors because of the expertise I have developed.

Learn how to apply these learnings in your own journey as you expand into your next level in life and in career. In every new experience, see it as an opportunity to discover more about yourself, what you like and don't like, what you enjoy doing and what doesn't fulfill you. Be curious about yourself and the world around you and utilize all of the skills you've gained and experiences you've had to your advantage. Take it all with you along every step of your journey and use it to your advantage. Those years you have spent in whatever industry you've dedicated yourself to are of great value not only to you but to every person you serve. Think about how much you have to give to others through all the years you've invested in learning your craft and how much of a jump start you can give someone else by giving them just one bit of advice from your insider knowledge.

REFLECTION >>>

Being forced to do it all can be seen as a problem, but the goal is to challenge yourself to see it as an opportunity. It is an opportunity to learn more about yourself, an opportunity to learn new things and an opportunity to be stretched to new levels of growth. Being an eternal learner can mean being an eternal leader. Having a good working knowledge in multiple areas is a desirable trait in a world where we are expected to do more, be more and know more.

1. Do you see "doing it all" as a challenge or an opportunity?

_____

_____

_____

_____

_____

_____

2. What skills have you learned that you are great at doing?

_____

_____

_____

_____

_____

_____

3. What advice can you give that would be of great value to someone else?

_____

_____

_____

_____

_____

_____

4. What tasks really feel like a chore?

_____

_____

_____

_____

_____

_____

CHAPTER 6

Who NEEDS an Agent

"Being ourselves means sometimes having to find the courage to stand alone, totally alone."

A t every stage of my journalism career, I succeeded at finding and securing my jobs without the help of an agent. In this industry, it is pretty common to get the support of an agent to help you find job openings, secure interviews, and negotiate contracts on your behalf. But the agent doesn't get paid until you get paid. You reach a level where in order to get your next job or promotion you need the support of someone else advocating on your behalf. After working in Houston, Texas, one of the top ten markets in the country for about a year, I decided I needed a change. The position I was in I felt wasn't allowing me to utilize all of my gifts and talents. Sure, I had won an award for my feature reports while working there, but I was not in a position that allowed me to be the kind of reporter I had set out to be. So like most mid-level journalists, I was toying with the idea of getting an agent. About that same time an agent based in North Carolina reached out to me through LinkedIn and expressed interest in representing me. Part of me was flattered; however, the other part of me questioned if I really needed an agent.

Like I said, up until this point I'd done it all on my own. I got my first gig right out of college at the age of twenty-one and quickly moved up to a mid-level market where I eventually became a weekend anchor. And now I was working in one of the largest news markets in the country; however, I was feeling a bit of disappointment after being turned down for several jobs that I was applying for at the time. So I took a call with the potential agent and heard him out to see if he would be a good fit for me and where I was trying to go in my career. Ultimately, my goal was to stay in the southern region and possibly land a job in my hometown of New Orleans. After several months of searching and applying, I wasn't getting anywhere. I signed an agreement to work with this agent in hopes of getting over this hurdle and to the next level of my career.

We worked together for several more months and he got me an in-person job interview in Columbus, Ohio, where I would've been a breaking news anchor on the morning news shows. I also had a phone interview with a news director at a station in Maine, a place I never once considered as a possibility nor ever wanted to move to. I'm not one to turn down an opportunity without considering it, so I interviewed for the job knowing full well it wasn't a place I could see myself living.

Then I landed an interview with a station in West Palm Beach. I'm a girl who loves fun in the sun and midday sunbathing, so this sounded like the place for me. I had an interview with the news director over the phone that went great. Then they invited me out for another interview at the station, and I fell in love with the city after spending just a day there. The last step was a writing test, which was a breeze. I went home feeling great about the visit and thinking this was going to be the place for me. Sure enough, I got the job! The only downside was when the offer came in, it was for $10,000 less than what I was making at the time. On top of that, I would have to pay the agency a percentage of those earnings. But who could say no to living on the beach and soaking up the sun? Here I was willing to accept less to do more work because I thought it was better than what I had, which was nothing. I had no other offers on the table after months of searching.

I put in my two weeks' notice at the station I was working at in Houston and was ready to pack up and move. Then as we got closer to the end of that two weeks, there was still no contract. The news director said they were working to finalize things with their corporate offices. To me that sounded like the job was not as secure as I thought. At that point, that tenacity from my old days kicked in, and I got to work for myself. I got on the phone with some of my old contacts at WDSU in New Orleans where I interned some years prior. I sent my good friend Kendal Francis, who has become like a big brother, my updated résumé tape and inquired about any possible openings at the station. He passed my information along to the assistant news director who apparently was in the process of looking for new reporters. He told me once the managers saw my material they were eager to bring me in for an interview! I immediately planned my trip back home for an interview that upcoming Friday. It went amazing! I met with the news director, connected with former co-workers and went to lunch with the general manager to seal the deal! After that I knew it was my time to go home, which had always been in my five-year plan, and here it was happening in real time.

At that point I just waited to hear the official word that I got the job. When I did, it was time to tell my agent that I no longer wanted to accept the position in West Palm Beach. When I delivered the news, it didn't go over so well with him. From his perspective I should've gotten him in on helping me negotiate a deal with WDSU in New Orleans. From my perspective, I didn't need his help getting a job in the first place so I figured I didn't need his help negotiating a deal that he didn't help me get either. Still he felt it was only fair that I still pay him for the salary he had negotiated for me in West Palm Beach. I agreed but was determined to cut ties once I finished paying the financial obligations. I'm sure I could have found some legal way to get out of paying him, but I didn't have the energy to fight him on it.

If this experience taught me anything it's that making and maintaining meaningful connections goes a long way and helps to advance your career and leverage you to the next level at every stage. Although I've had a number of jobs in my fourteen-year news career, one thing I am proud to say is that

I could easily go back to any of those previous jobs because of my reputation, work ethic and diligence in maintaining a strong network of connections and friendships.

Building that network has also been vital to my success as a media coach and consultant. People in this line of work uproot and move frequently. News people are nomadic folk setting up shop in new cities every two to three years until they ultimately reach their final landing place or reach what they deem as the pinnacle of their career. The network I've built is now an asset to help me get my clients the media attention they may be seeking. It makes it so easy to connect with old colleagues wherever they are whether it be in DC, Orlando, New York, LA, Houston or any place in between.

Back to my return to New Orleans, when I finally made it home in November 2012, it felt like a homecoming; family, friends, anyone I knew was ecstatic to know they could watch me on the news in my hometown. It was an amazing journey, even if there was a bit of an acclimation having been gone from home for a bit. I remember my first time on air, I actually used the station call letters from one of my old stations. There were some nerves I had to shake being on TV in front of an audience of people who actually knew me. I also had to adjust to being back on air full-time seeing as for the past year I wasn't a reporter on a full-time basis. But if you know anything at all about New Orleans, the people and its culture, it's that they all have a way of making you feel like family or a friend you've known for years. They welcomed me home like I never left. I also had to readjust to the local colloquialisms like calling the trolley a streetcar and calling the median a neutral ground. Believe me, if I messed these things up on air or mispronounced the name of the street, the audience was sure to let me and the new station know with a sharply worded email.

As you are advancing in your career or maybe working to start your own business, lean into your network and the connections you have made. Think of the macro connections in your network who you can directly reach out to as a resource, whether it be to help you get the promotion you've been seeking, start your non-profit, generate new clients, gain access to funding, or even access to a room that you know if you show up in, you can do what it takes to close a deal. Who are the micro connections around you that can help connect you to the decision makers and who can put in a good word for you as you're looking to advance. If you've done great work and leave a lasting impression on those you've worked with or encountered in your life, all of the people you've come into contact with can serve as the connection to help you reach the next step in your career and journey.

REFLECTION

When you truly understand and know your worth, you know what you deserve and what makes your heart sing. You also trust yourself to make the decisions that best serve you and believe in your ability to figure things out on your own. You don't get down on yourself when hard times hit. Instead, you remind yourself how strong you are and keep on going and moving forward toward your purpose and goals. You don't settle, so you never wake one day regretting and wondering what could have been.

1. In what areas of your life are you settling for less?

_____

_____

_____

_____

_____

2. Where can you trust yourself to do for yourself without relying on others?

_____

_____

_____

_____

_____

3. What decisions need to be made to best serve you?

_____

_____

_____

_____

_____

4. Who are the people who can be your connectors?

_____

_____

_____

_____

_____

CHAPTER 7

My HAIR Story

"I've learned that people will forget what you said, people will forget what you did, but people will never forget how you made them feel."-Maya Angelou

When I started working in the news industry, I went into it with the idea that I had to have a certain look to be accepted in mainstream media. Since I was fresh out of college, I also wanted my appearance to make me look more mature so I would be respected and seen as a serious reporter by viewers. So I cut my hair into a short straight bob, which was a pretty popular style on the news at the time. I maintained that hairstyle for years because there is also an expectation for women in news to look the same and not change their appearance often. Our bosses and consultants say we have to keep our looks consistent so it doesn't confuse the viewer or have them paying more attention to our appearance and new hair than the story we're sharing.

While I was working in Shreveport between 2008-2011, I started to try different things with my hair like dying it, adding highlights or even doing a more updated version of my anchor bob. After working there for close to two years I decided to stop getting a relaxer, which is the chemical process used to straighten black women's hair.. I had been getting a relaxer since the age of nine when I was in fourth grade. My grandmother would apply the creamy concoction to my hair regularly every six to eight weeks right there in her kitchen. It was a regular routine for me and my mom to get a relaxer so our hair could be long, flowy and straight. I never really questioned it; it was just something that we did. Even when I went off to college, I managed to still get my relaxer whether it was while on break at home or on occasion finding a stylist in Dallas who would do it for me.

My stylist in Shreveport was the person who first encouraged me to stop getting relaxers. She walked me through the year-long process to grow out my relaxer, so I was going to her almost every two weeks to get my hair flat ironed so I didn't look any different on air. With her support, I was able to make the transition beautifully in real life and on-air. Although I never wore my natural curls on air at the time, it felt amazing to finally make a personal choice for me and my health that I was proud of even if it was my little secret. By the time I was preparing to make my next career move to Houston, Texas in 2011, we decided to cut off all of the straight ends and do my first big chop! I was excited about doing it, but let's just say I didn't quite like how my hair looked after the cut. I was just so accustomed to seeing it long and straight for all those years.

When I did make it to Houston, although I wasn't working as an on-air reporter, I still felt a bit self-conscious about my new short style. During those years most of the women around me at my job and throughout the city were rocking long, straight weaves, so I succumbed to the pressures of my environment and got a weave sewed in for the very first time. I was never a fan of sew-ins, but I thought I'd give it a try. Let's just say I was underwhelmed with the experience. Although the stylist did an amazing job, again here I was with a hairstyle that just didn't feel like me. I kept it in for a couple of months because it was a big investment, and to let my hair grow out a bit more. Once I took the weave out, I started wearing my curls, my natural curls for the first time since I was a little girl. It was a new experience and it felt so nice to embrace wearing my own hair without the extensions. I maintained it like that for about eight more months until I got my new job as an on-air reporter in New Orleans.

Since I was going to be back in an on-air TV role, I regretfully decided to get a relaxer again because in my mind that's still what I had to do to be on TV. While working in New Orleans, I tried a variety of hairstyles. I had highlights, extensions and even had red hair at one point. The red hair was not a hit among my male bosses who literally asked me to tone it down a bit, but when I was out in the field reporting, the ladies loved it. You'd be surprised how many more people are willing to talk to the reporter with the red hair when you're out on a crime scene.

My hair was always a topic of conversation throughout my career. I remember early on while at a journalism convention an older gentleman who was critiquing my work told me, "Your hair is too long, and middle-aged women won't want you in their living rooms on their TV because they wouldn't want their husbands watching you." I thought that was the most absurd thing I've ever heard but realized that was the belief system the journalism profession had operated under for years and it's what I was indoctrinated to believe as well.

Women were subjected to an unrealistic and unwanted code of conduct when it came to our appearance, from what we wear to how we do our hair. The level of sexism and ageism is unreal. Men are not held to the same standards. Men can sit at an anchor desk until they're old and gray and women are shuffled out the door before menopause! A man could wear the same suit for a year and no one would notice. In fact, in 2014 an Australian news anchor did just that to prove this point. Karl Stefanovic wore the same navy suit every day for a year, and not one viewer reported that they noticed. The *Today* program anchor called it an experiment to highlight sexism and said it was a show of solidarity for his co-anchor who is judged more harshly for what she wears.

In a way, I believe I kept making changes to my hair to prove a point. Not only was I tired of having to wear my hair the same way all the time, but I also wanted to prove that I was great at my job no matter what my hair looked like. My appearance does not determine my talent.

In 2016, with the help of my stylist at the time, who was my cousin Christi Pallagao, I decided to transition back to wearing my natural hair.

Throughout the yearlong process, we gradually cut my hair shorter and shorter until all of it was curly, but we were still straightening it with hot tools almost weekly. Then my hair had gotten so short to the point that I could no longer straighten it myself at home. On a Monday morning in May, I woke up to get ready for work after spending the Sunday before at the New Orleans Jazz and Heritage Festival. It was a day full of dancing, singing and having fun with friends in the heat. I went to sleep that night without doing anything to protect my hair. When I woke up, I looked like a peacock and I couldn't do anything to fix the massive mess on my head. I immediately decided it would be the day that I wore my natural hair on TV. I got in the shower, washed my hair and put some products on my curls and went to work that day ready to reveal my new look to the world.

I remember the day so vividly but didn't realize at the time how transformative that split decision would be in my life. I didn't put much consideration into it—I just did it. That day I covered a story about children shooting paintball guns at residents and homes in the Bywater neighborhood of New Orleans. It was very rare for me to get pictures of myself working in the field and it just so happened that day someone in the neighborhood took pictures of me and a photojournalist interviewing people. I'm so glad to have those pictures to document a day that marked a major change in my life and my hair journey.

Now almost daily I get compliments on my hair and my curls, which have grown out past my shoulders. Women are always seeking advice on which products to use for their hair, what stylists to go to and how to care for their or their daughter's natural curls. It has been so amazing for me to learn how foreign it is for some women to care for their natural hair. For so long black women have felt the need or the desire to alter our hair and our appearance based on societal pressures and Eurocentric standards of beauty. So much so that we no longer know how to care for our natural hair or appreciate the hair we were born with.

My hair journey also became the impetus for me to write a children's book titled *Curly Girl: My Curls Are Mine to Love.* The book is about a little girl named Baylee who absolutely loves her big curly poofs until her schoolmates make fun of her hair. After the first day of school, to her mom's surprise, Baylee wants to change her hair. That was until she saw something on television that made her love her curls like never before- a news reporter with curly hair like her. I published the book several years after meeting a seven-year-old girl named Lyndee at an event I was hosting. She had the most amazing curly hair and bubbly personality, and even asked me for my phone number before we left the event that night. It was the funniest thing and I never forgot that moment. The book and the character, Baylee, were born out of that experience and so many others

I had with young girls and women who were so inspired by seeing a black woman with natural hair on the news.

There were women I looked up to as a young girl who fueled my desire to become a journalist. Growing up and watching women like Oprah Winfrey, Soledad O'Brien, Michelle Miller, Nischelle Turner, Hoda Kotb and Sally Ann Roberts on TV was proof to me that I could do it too. They inspired me in more ways than I realized until I was in the position to inspire curly girls everywhere to embrace the beauty of their natural hair just by living in my truth and pursuing my passion. Imagine the full circle moments and joy I had when I was able to put my book into the hands of Nischelle Turner, Michelle Miller, Hoda Kotb and Sally Anny Roberts and share with them how much they meant to me as a young girl and as a journalist following in their footsteps. I still have to get a copy of the book to Soledad and Oprah to complete this full circle.

Cutting my hair was truly transformational. It was like I was accepting myself and letting go of something I was so attached to. I had been on a journey that made me more self-aware and developed on a personal level, which in turn helped me in all aspects of my life. Cutting my hair was the starting point for me to break free from the past and move into the present.

Studies have shown that cutting your hair, especially when going through a traumatic life change, can provide a sense of control and emotional release. Changing one's hairstyle can also be a powerful tool in helping redefine or solidify one's identity.

But, why is simply cutting your hair so freeing? It helps us embrace another side of ourselves during trying times. Cutting our hair is also an easy way to achieve instant gratification. When everything feels like it's falling apart, we can have some control over our new look. And it acts as a sort of release.

This perfectly describes the place I was in personally and in my career. I was ready to move on from the news business, but felt tied to it as part of my identity. I thought this is who everyone knows me as and this is who they expect me to be, but it wasn't who I wanted to be any longer. Cutting my hair was the start of me moving to this place of limbo and feeling trapped. I even felt my reporting became better because I felt so much more like myself and not this cookie cutter image of what a reporter is. I felt like I was finally living in my truth and my hair was the outward expression of what I was feeling inside. It helped me find my true identity and voice as a reporter and set me on my journey to live in my truth in other ways.

When you take a look at where you are in your life and career and really do an assessment, is there anything that you feel is holding you back from achieving your goals? Is there something that is keeping you stuck in your past or that has you afraid to take a detour? Do you feel like you have to keep charging down the road you're on because this is how you've always done it, this is who everyone sees you as or this is just what you're expected to do? Who says you can't reroute, take that detour to explore something new and follow that instinct inside of you telling you there has to be something better than this. I encourage you to listen to that still tiny voice in your head that is urging you to take a step in a new direction because that next step just might be the best step to push you in the direction of rediscovering you and reconnecting with your passion.

REFLECTION »»

You must understand that your worth and who you are is not based on external factors but is rooted in the qualities, gifts and talents you have to offer the world. Getting to the core of who you are and living in your truth opens up a new level of personal strength, conviction and self-knowledge. Rather than live by the standards and expectations placed upon you by society, live by the standards that hold true to your personal values.

1. What standards are you placing on yourself based on the ideas of others?

    _____

    _____

    _____

2. What unrealistic expectations are you attempting to live up to?

    _____

    _____

    _____

3. What changes can you make to more closely align with living as your true self?

    _____

    _____

    _____

CHAPTER 8

Getting Out of the BOX

"A full stop followed by an involuntary reflection occurs when life changes from fast to slow."

can't tell you how many stories I have reported on since starting my career in 2007. There were several that changed the trajectory of my career, life and mindset in 2017. In January of that year, there was a man threatening to jump from the Crescent City Connection Bridge over the Mississippi River in New Orleans. The man was there for hours, traffic was at a standstill and people in town and in my newsroom started wishing he'd just jump to "get it over with."

At that point I realized how callous and jaded people could be. But I also realized how desensitized I had become to tragedy after a decade in the news business. I have seen so many dead bodies carted into the back of a coroner's van and interviewed way too many mothers and family members after their loved ones were murdered or killed in a tragedy. Much like the police, news reporters are among the first responders at shooting scenes, house fires and natural disasters, and that began to weigh heavily on me.

Then in February 2017, I was covering a tornado hitting a neighborhood of New Orleans. My photographer and I were literally on the interstate headed east in anticipation of the bad weather when it touched down on a highway about a mile away from us. We ended up hiding inside a stranger's damaged house because our weather team was worried another tornado would come our way. It was then that I realized not only was I putting my safety and my life at risk for the sake of a two-minute news story, but I was not doing what I thought I would be doing in this career. I was not in a position to really highlight the positivity happening in communities all over the country every day.

Later that year, I remember being in a performance evaluation with two of my supervisors and they asked me why I rarely came to the morning editorial meeting with news story ideas. I don't know what came over me but I just blurted out, "Because I'm not passionate about it anymore." They both looked at each other with a bit of confusion, probably thinking, did she really just say that, is she serious? There weren't any follow-up questions after I said that. I think we all knew at that moment that my time there would be coming to an end soon.

By that time, I clearly showed my lack of desire to stay in the news business. I was reluctant to sign long-term contracts and repeatedly signed six-month extensions. The pull inside of me to shift into a new direction was growing stronger and

I could no longer ignore it. In May of 2017, I officially put in my last two week notice. That was only three weeks after I made the shift to wearing my natural curls on the news. I was at a pivotal point in my life and career and the next few months would set the stage for the next chapter.

I made a full stop leaving my full-time job as a news reporter after more than a decade in the business and put a lot of time and energy into doing the work on myself. That meant working with a success coach to eliminate negative self-talk, examining myself to identify my passion and purpose, looking for areas of strength and weakness, and just being real with others and myself.

There has been an enormous amount of change in my life since then as I have evolved as a woman and professional. When I nailed down my purpose and got clear on who I am here to serve, I began to see change and it had a beautiful impact on my life and on the lives of others.

It did not come without me having a bit of an identity crisis. I was still trying to figure out who I was outside of my profession and what people knew me as. I was struggling with the feeling of not being relevant or useful if I wasn't on television every day anymore. But I also knew I was feeling unfulfilled, uninspired and my heart was no longer in the profession I'd dedicated so many years of my life to. I was burnt out from telling stories about murder, hurt and pain felt by so many in my community. I wanted to focus on more of the positive things within the city I love, so I stepped away to pursue other opportunities.

As time went on I began to feel renewed, more confident about my career choices and more free to be the new me I was becoming and discovering new things about myself. I was able to take everything I learned and experienced as a journalist to help people learn how to strategically get the media attention they were seeking. THIS is what can happen when you say YES to yourself and your passions. Feeling real joy and peace in life is something that I've wanted and now feel I have.

I've been able to LEVERAGE my 13-year career in the news business, and I'm now the CEO of my own media coaching and consulting business where I get to work with business owners and nonprofits that feel stuck and lack guidance by giving them a road map and strategies to effectively share their story and gain media attention to grow their business visibility.

So how can YOU take all your life experience and expertise and leverage that into creating the life you dream of and living in your purpose? It starts with "Remembering your WHY!" Research suggests that people who have a sense of purpose in life live longer, and this is also linked to a person's quality of life and to better physical and mental health generally.

That's why remembering your WHY is so important. It's instrumental in staying focused and not letting everyday life tasks and the needs of others get in the way of you pursuing and achieving your goals and feeling accomplished in life. To reach that point you have to be dedicated to your mission and be passionate about what it is you do because it may not be glamorous and may not always be gratifying. In the midst of all the negativity in the world and possibly around you, you may lose sight of your WHY. WHY do you do this work? WHY you've committed years of your life to this job. WHY you lie awake at night with those thoughts, ideas and dreams weighing on you.

Knowing your WHY is one of the most important things you can figure out in your life. Your WHY is the reason you get out of bed in the morning and do all that you do. Your WHY is your purpose, what you believe you are meant to do in life. Some of us know our WHY, some of us don't and for some of us it changes over the course of a lifetime. Knowing your purpose in life, and in this season of your life, is so crucial because it gives you direction. It allows you to focus, to prioritize and to let go of what isn't serving that purpose.

We all need to remember our WHY and come back to that on a regular basis, to check in with yourself no matter where you are on your journey. Are you on track and living a fulfilling life or did you get lost and need to find your way back? When you let your WHY guide your decisions you can be confident you are making the right decisions even if they are hard sometimes.

When we're living an unconscious life where we never think of our WHY, it leaves us feeling lost and without a purpose.

Do you know your WHY?

My purpose is to live with integrity and communicate my story authentically to encourage women to discover their own inner peace and purpose. I try to infuse everything I do

with my WHY and let it guide how I am building my business and my life.

I started revamping my life and career and creating my
own lane for one main reason! To feel freedom! Freedom looks
completely different for everyone. For one person it may be
waking up early and going for a run before tackling the day's
tasks. For another it could mean being your own boss.

For me, freedom has meant being able to explore all of my
talents, gifts and passions on my own terms and not feeling
stuck. It means being able to say no to some job offers and
saying yes to the things that I really want to do! It means
choosing my personal happiness over a salary from a career
that left me feeling unfulfilled. It means prioritizing the people
in my life who matter to me. It means taking charge of my
journey and not being who others expect me to be, really
being my authentic self and doing the things that truly bring
me joy. It means being able to use my passion for storytelling
and journalism by exploring new ways of doing it. It means
fully loving myself and allowing myself to fully and freely
love someone else without questions, doubts or concerns! It's
my belief that we all have a story worth telling. The secret is
identifying the parts of your story that make YOU unique!

Sometimes the most challenging part of this journey is
figuring out the answers to these questions, "What do I have
to offer," "What makes me special," or "Why should anyone
care about what I have to say?" This is something the reporter
in me is great at helping people figure out and something I
help my clients do all the time.

REFLECTON >>>

Sometimes you have to stop doing what you've always done to reach the next level in your life or career, to unlock your full potential and unlock everything that's inside of you. It doesn't mean you have to forget everything you've ever known but instead use it to build something new. That's the key to unlocking your passions is to identify and fill your day with what energizes you. What you DO must be in alignment with what you WANT TO DO.

1. What would it mean to you to have my own business or the income I really want?

_____

_____

_____

_____

_____

_____

2. If you could start a business today, what would it be?

_____

_____

_____

_____

_____

_____

3. Write out a clear, honest vision of what running your business means to you and what you ultimately want to achieve.

_____

_____

_____

_____

_____

_____

CHAPTER 9

Write Your OWN Story

Just as I was beginning to grow my business and stand on my own two feet, the world changed and I was faced with another "full stop." In February 2020, I accepted a position as the Communications Director and Corporate Event Coordinator for a new entertainment complex. Only weeks ahead of the grand opening, I was hired to spearhead the festivities to celebrate the new business and start to generate media attention around the business. We were successful in getting reporters there from all the local news stations and newspapers. There was even a viral video of the mayor dancing on one of the arcade games and council members engaged in a competitive bumper car session. With all the media attention, people we piling in to schedule parties for birthday parties and business was great. This gave me more confidence that I was actually pretty good in this new line of work. It was a short-lived excitement because it all came to a screeching halt 37 days later.

News about COVID-19 began to spread and we were forced to close the business due to local lockdowns. What was expected to be a two-week lockdown turned into months of me sitting at home with no clear end in sight. The COVID-19 pandemic forced me to further reevaluate. I eventually made a return to the news and started doing freelance reporting to support my old news station, but to also maintain my sanity during this uncertain time. Throughout the first year of the pandemic, I also spent countless hours and invested thousands of dollars in working with several success and business coaches to figure out my way forward. During this time, I finally completed and was able to work toward publishing my first children's book, "Curly Girl: My Curls are Mine to Love." Keep reading for more on that exciting launch.

I was eventually no longer able to wait for work to pick back up at the entertainment center with the pandemic lockdowns pressing on and PPP funding running out. By January of 2021, I was five months pregnant and needed to find ways to contribute financially as my husband and I had just moved into a new home. Soon an opportunity came along for me to become the Communications Manager with a local non-profit called STEM NOLA where I worked closely with the CEO to build out a complete communications team and share the organization's work with media locally and nationally. Just as I was getting into the groove of things, my son was ready to enter the world.

His born day was full of big deliveries, as I was also scheduled to have the launch for my new children's book! As I was on a zoom call with a friend preparing for the big night, my contractions started. Instead of attending my book launch in person, I had to zoom in from my hospital bed to say hello to everyone who showed up as I was having the "epidural shakes." Then two hours later he was born. While you may expect this may have led to another full stop, it was the complete opposite for me. My son was born two weeks early on a Thursday, and by that Sunday, I was headed home and had just booked a role in a feature film called, "National Champions." Two weeks after giving birth, my son, mom and I were on a movie set in a hotel in downtown New Orleans. I somehow had enough energy to spend the entire day on set and he was getting his regular breast feedings while I waited to shoot my scene.

My son's birth was also followed up by a virtual book tour to promote my book because of course I couldn't lose the momentum of having just launched my first book. When I did return to work eight weeks later, I was promoted to the Director of Communications and received a nice bump in my pay. I guess my absence was felt and the work I produced was worth the promotion and raise. After nearly two years with the non-profit, I started to get restless again and wanted to explore other growth opportunities. I was also starting to grow my business on the side, and my earnings in my "side business" started to catch up with my earnings from my full-time job.

In August of that year, I hired a marketing company to really help me build my brand and grow my visibility online and social media, and with all the word of mouth referrals, my business began to earn me more than my salary. That was a clear indication that I was really on to something and I became adamant about wanting to be in a new position that was going to pay me my reputation for success and results for my clients was starting to get noticed in places I didn't even realize. I was being recruited for jobs left and right and even turned down a 6-figure offer because it just didn't feel right for me.

Then in November of 2022, I got a call from someone asking if I would be interested in running communications for her organization, but I didn't actually recognize the voice or the name of the person calling. It was the newly elected sheriff of the Orleans Parish, Susan Hutson. I had never met her before, nor did I know she was the sheriff when I answered the call. I was googling her name to figure it out when I finally just asked, "what organization are you with." When she told me, it was a complete surprise because I certainly wasn't expecting the call. Apparently, I had come highly recommended by some of her associates and a judge who knows me well.

I scheduled a meeting with the sheriff and her chief of staff and prepared a full presentation to show her what me and my team could do for her and the department. I went in there with three of my colleagues, all men, and all the confidence in the world ready to land my first big contract. I knew as a woman in charge herself, she appreciated how I commanded the room and led my team through the presentation. I also knew I had the advantage of being the only person she invited into that room to discuss this opportunity. When we left the conference room, the chief of staff pulled me aside and said "she really just wants you." I replied jokingly, "If you can get me $120,000, then I'll consider it." I should add that by this point, I had been recruited by the New Orleans Police Department, the New Orleans Mayor's Office and a national PR Firm to work in their communications departments, and I either didn't get hired for whatever reason or I declined the opportunities. After meeting the sheriff, I knew I could provide support on improving the agency's communications and help to shield some of the negative press she was receiving since taking office. I could also tell they would benefit from having someone on staff managing the communications rather than a contractor.

A week later, I was receiving the offer letter with a salary well above what I even asked for and benefits that made the offer too good to turn down. The Chief of Staff later told me they didn't have time to go through all the negotiations, so they were offering me top dollar to get me in the door so I could get to work. I spoke to some of my mentors and colleagues about the opportunity I was presented with and some of them discouraged me from taking it. While I understood their per-spectives, I saw this as an opportunity to finally be in a position that would give me the freedom I'd been looking to achieve. Ultimately, I decided to accept the position because it was an opportunity to stretch myself in this new lane I was paving and it allowed me to grow as a leader and professional. If I've learned anything from this experience it's these three things:

Your work and reputation will speak for you!

My talent and commitment to my work got me in a door I wasn't even trying to enter. People were recommending me for a job I was not aware was available. By simply doing my work, and being good at what I do, I built a reputation that helped to get me in the door to unlock my next big opportunity.

You are enough!

Hearing the Chief of Staff say, "the sheriff just wants you," helped remind me that I am enough. I believe that! You are enough, flaws, imperfections and all. If you are consistent in doing great work, continuing to show up, grow and develop in your field, you are enough.

Name Your Price and ASK FOR IT!

While I have the support of so many around me, what I've learned is that people really just want to work with me. That means I can name my price then add tax and the people who really want to work with me will pay it because I have the proven results. I am worth every investment I've made into myself, and every investment is paying off for me.

When building your business, there will likely be life experiences, parts of your past, or maybe even traumas you overcame that became the impetus for you wanting to start your business. Those are the things that make YOU and your business unique. Those life experiences, your expertise and those things you have overcome are the backbone of your business. It's how you use those things to drive you that is the key to Leveraging YOU.

I truly believe that every person has an INNER DESIRE begging to be free. This DESIRE is what leads many people to look within, to become the person they were destined to be. They take their life experiences, good and bad, to LEVERAGE them into their own GREATNESS.

I know all too well the mindset of a woman who wanted more but just didn't know what that more was or how to get to it. But one thing I knew was I wanted MORE! I wanted to be free to follow my heart SO I....

- Left a full-time job as a television reporter after 10 years in the business…
- Started doing freelance work…
- Was making maybe half the $52,000 salary I once earned
- Lived off my parents for a time (gratefully) and relied on them for housing, cell phone service and other basic necessities...
- Started searching for real jobs to make ends meet…
- Got interviews, but no one hired me…Kept going back and forth to a job I didn't really want to do anymore...

THEN IT CLICKED!!!

I'm not getting where I want in life professionally, personally or financially because I'm doing the same old things expecting different results. I left a career because I said I wanted more, but I wasn't getting more out of life because I was not putting in the work to get there. I know all too well the mindset of a woman who wanted more but just didn't know what that more was or how to get to it. But one thing I knew was I wanted MORE! I wanted to be free to follow my heart.

My point in sharing this is to show you that to get the most out of life, you have to do more, be more and work more for yourself. It's time to dig down deep and take all that energy you're putting toward building someone else's dreams and stop spinning your wheels and getting nowhere. You have to put energy toward creating the life you DESERVE and DESIRE. But it takes getting real with yourself and taking on the challenge of discovering the REAL YOU.

Now let's get back to answering those crucial questions we presented in the last chapter. The questions about what I have to offer, what makes you special and why should anyone care what you have to say. I want to help you discover the unlocked potential inside and identify your Secret Sauce!

The "Secret Sauce" is no secret because the secret sauce is YOU! It's the parts of your life that shape you, drive you and make you who you are. Various aspects of your life-- the experiences, your challenges, things you've overcome, your wins, your achievements, your training-- that all make up parts of your existence and personal story.

LET'S DISCOVER YOUR SECRET SAUCE!

1. Write out everything that makes you special, unique & different:

_____

_____

_____

_____

_____

2. Ask yourself these questions as you discover your secret sauce.

_____

_____

_____

_____

_____

3. What do people ask you about the most?

_____

_____

_____

_____

_____

4. What problems do you solve for people naturally without thinking twice about the solution?

_____

_____

_____

_____

_____

5. What experiences have you had in your life that can help you easily solve someone else's problem?

_____

_____

_____

_____

_____

READY TO UNLOCK YOUR SECRET SAUCE?

Now that I've given you some steps to unlock your secret sauce, it's time to take some action!

I want to make it easier for you to take the next steps to unlock your secret sauce by joining Leverage You Academy!

Leverage You isn't just about gaining confidence; it's about becoming the authority you were destined to be. Your expertise, your story, and your life experiences are your secret sauce – and it's time to unlock the full flavor.

As a valued member of my community, I'm excited to offer you a special gift so you can get started today! Use the code "GrowWithCasey" for 50% off all Leverage You Academy courses.
https://bit.ly/leverageYOU

ABOUT THE AUTHOR

Connect with Casey

Email - casey@caseyferrand.com

Website - https://www.caseyferrand.com

Instagram - @caseyferrandmcgee

Facebook - https://www.facebook.com/CaseyFerrand

Casey Ferrand McGee is an award winning journalist and children's fiction author, entrepreneur and public relations strategist who has had a love for storytelling ever since she was a little girl. Casey writes because she loves to share her story and knowledge with others, to inspire them to pursue their passion and leverage their knowledge and experience to build a life they love.

Casey lives in New Orleans with her husband and son where she dines on creole cuisine and enjoys traveling to new cities where she often finds herself tuning into the local news.

She writes children's fiction books and non-fiction books about personal development, navigating career and entrepreneurship and offers coaching to help people tap into the media to grow their business or brand.

Casey Ferrand McGee has a television and media career spanning more than 20 years, from her years as a child actress in New Orleans to her career as a nationally award-winning journalist. As the Owner of CFM Media, Casey provides media coaching, public relations and production services to CEO's, Founders, Executives, Public Officials, Business Owners and organizations. She specializes in a special style of writing and storytelling that enhances the profile of leaders helping them gain media attention that shines a spotlight on their work and experience.